CHAPTER 1.
MOMENTUM
INVESTING
PHILOSOPHY

"Momentum investing is a strategy that has been proven over time and is backed by extensive academic research. We believe that momentum is a powerful force in the market and that investors who can identify and capitalize on these trends can generate attractive returns."

Ken Griffin

Momentum investing is a popular investment strategy that involves buying stocks that have shown strong performance in the past and holding onto them for a period of time. The idea behind this strategy is that stocks that have shown momentum in the past are likely to continue performing well in the future. One stock that exemplifies the concept of momentum investing is Tesla Inc. (TSLA).

Tesla is a leading electric vehicle (EV) manufacturer that has been at the forefront of the EV revolution. The company was founded in 2003 by entrepreneur Elon Musk, with the aim of accelerating the transition to sustainable energy. Since its inception, Tesla has been a disruptive force in the automotive industry, and has quickly established itself as a leader in the EV space.

Tesla's stock has been on a remarkable run in recent years, driven by a combination of strong financial performance and investor optimism about the company's future prospects. The stock has been one of the best-performing stocks in the market, with a year-to-date (YTD) return of over 100% as of April 2023. This strong performance has attracted the attention of momentum investors, who are looking to capitalize on the stock's upward trend.

One of the key drivers of Tesla's momentum has been its strong financial performance. The company has consistently reported strong revenue growth and has been profitable for several quarters in a row. In the fourth quarter of 2022, Tesla reported revenue of $17.4 billion, up 98% year-over-year. The company also reported earnings per share (EPS) of $2.93, beating analysts' expectations.

Another factor driving Tesla's momentum is the company's strong brand and leadership position in the EV market. Tesla is widely recognized as the leading EV manufacturer in the world, and has a loyal following of customers and investors. The company has also demonstrated a commitment to innovation, with a strong focus on research and development, which has helped it stay ahead of its competitors.

Momentum investors are attracted to stocks like Tesla because they believe that the stock's upward momentum will continue in the future. This is based on the idea that stocks that have performed well in the past are likely to continue performing well, at least for a certain period of time. Momentum investors typically hold onto their positions for a few weeks or months, and then sell when the stock's momentum begins to wane.

However, momentum investing does carry some risks. One of the biggest risks is that the momentum can suddenly shift, causing the stock to decline rapidly. This can happen if there is a sudden shift in market sentiment, or if there is a negative news event that affects the stock's fundamentals. Investors who are considering momentum investing should be aware of these risks and should be prepared to exit their positions quickly if the momentum shifts.

One of the key differences between momentum investing and other investment principles is that momentum investing focuses exclusively on past performance rather than the fundamentals of a company. This means that momentum investors are less concerned with factors such as a company's financial health, earnings growth, or valuation, and more interested in the trend of the stock price.

Another difference between momentum investing and other investment principles is that momentum investing tends to be a shorter-term strategy. Momentum investors typically hold onto a stock for a few months to a year before selling it and moving onto another stock that has shown momentum.

In contrast, other investment strategies such as value investing or growth investing tend to be longer-term strategies. Value investors focus on buying stocks that are undervalued by the market and holding onto them until the market recognizes their true value. Growth investors, on the other hand, focus on companies with strong earnings growth potential and hold onto those stocks for a longer period of time.

Momentum investing can also be contrasted with contrarian investing, which involves buying stocks that have fallen out of favor with the market in the hopes that they will eventually rebound. Contrarian investors tend to take a longer-term approach, as they often have to wait for the market to recognize the value of the stocks they have purchased.

There are several key indicators that momentum investors use to identify stocks with strong momentum. These indicators can help investors determine whether a stock is likely to continue performing well in the future:

1. Price momentum: One of the primary indicators of momentum investing is price momentum, which is a measure of a stock's price movement over time. Momentum investors look for stocks that have shown a strong upward trend in their stock price over the past few months or years. This upward momentum can be measured using technical analysis tools such as moving averages or trend lines.

2. Relative strength: Another key indicator for momentum investors is relative strength, which measures how well a stock has performed compared to other stocks in its industry or sector. Stocks with high relative strength have outperformed their peers over a certain time period and are likely to continue outperforming in the future.

3. Earnings momentum: In addition to price momentum, momentum investors also look at earnings momentum, which measures a company's earnings growth rate over time. Companies with strong earnings momentum are likely to continue growing their earnings and may see their stock price rise as a result.

4. Volume: Momentum investors also look at trading volume to determine whether a stock has strong momentum. Stocks with high trading volume indicate that there is a lot of interest in the stock and that investors are buying and selling the stock frequently.

5. Analyst ratings: Investors may also consider analyst ratings and recommendations when identifying stocks with strong momentum. If a stock is receiving positive ratings from analysts and has a high price target, it may be a good candidate for momentum

investing.

CHAPTER 2.
WILLIAM O'NEIL

"The moral of the story is: never argue with the market. Your health and peace of mind are always more important than any stock."

William O'Neil

William O'Neil was born on March 25, 1933, in Oklahoma City, Oklahoma. His family moved to California when he was a child, and he grew up in Pasadena. As a teenager, O'Neil was interested in business and investing. He began investing in stocks at the age of 21 with just $500 he had saved from working odd jobs.

In 1958, O'Neil founded his first company, the O'Neil Data Systems. The company specialized in providing research data for stockbrokers and institutional investors. O'Neil's unique approach to data analysis and stock market research quickly gained the attention of the financial industry. He started the investment newsletter, Investor's Business Daily (IBD) in 1963. The publication's main focus was on providing investors with data and analysis to help them make informed investment decisions. IBD quickly became one of the most popular investment newsletters in the country.

During the 1970s, O'Neil's reputation as an investment expert continued to grow. He became a regular guest on television and radio shows, offering his insights on the stock market and investing.

His investment philosophy revolves around the concept of buying stocks that show strong momentum in their price and earnings growth. He uses a combination of technical and fundamental analysis to identify stocks that have strong momentum, and he places a strong emphasis on cutting losses quickly if a stock's momentum begins to weaken. Here is a step-by-step guide explaining how William O'Neil invests in stocks:

1. Look for Companies with Strong Fundamentals: His approach to investing starts with identifying companies with strong fundamentals, such as high earnings growth, high return on equity (ROE), and low debt-to-equity ratios. He believes that companies with strong fundamentals are more likely to outperform the market over the long term.

2. Identify Industry Groups with Strong Momentum: After identifying companies with strong fundamentals, O'Neil looks for industry groups that are showing strong momentum. He believes that investing in industry groups that are in an uptrend is more likely to result in higher returns. He uses IBD's proprietary industry group rankings to identify industry groups with strong momentum.

3. Look for Stocks with Strong Technicals: Once O'Neil has identified industry groups with strong momentum, he looks for individual stocks within those groups that are showing strong technicals. He uses a combination of chart patterns, such as cup-and-handle, double bottom, and flat base, to identify stocks that are poised to make a big move.

4. Check the Market Direction: Before making any trades, he checks the overall market direction to ensure that the market is in an uptrend. He uses IBD's proprietary market trend indicators to assess the

overall health of the market.

5. Buy Stocks with Strong Technicals and Fundamentals: Once O'Neil has identified stocks with strong technicals and fundamentals, he waits for a proper buy point to enter the trade. He uses a combination of chart patterns and technical indicators, such as moving averages and relative strength, to identify the optimal time to buy.

6. Monitor Stocks Closely: After entering a trade, he closely monitors the stock's performance and adjusts his position accordingly. He uses a combination of stop-loss orders and profit targets to manage risk and maximize returns.

7. Sell Stocks that are Underperforming: If a stock is not performing as expected, O'Neil will sell the position and move on to other opportunities. He believes in cutting losses quickly and moving on to the next trade.

In the early 1980s, Walmart was a relatively unknown discount retailer that was trading at a low valuation. However, William O'Neil saw the potential for the company to grow and become a dominant player in the retail industry. He believed that Walmart's low-cost business model and focus on customer service would enable it to outperform its competitors over the long term.

O'Neil's investment in Walmart was based on a combination of fundamental and technical analysis. He recognized that Walmart had strong fundamentals, such as high earnings growth, high return on equity (ROE), and low debt-to-equity ratios. He also saw that the company was expanding rapidly, with plans to open new stores across the country. This combination of strong fundamentals and growth potential made Walmart an attractive investment opportunity.

In addition to fundamental analysis, O'Neil also used technical analysis to identify the optimal time to buy Walmart's stock. He saw that the stock was trading in a tight range and was showing signs of accumulation by institutional investors. This was a bullish sign that suggested that the stock was poised for a breakout.

His investment in Walmart was not without risk. At the time, the retail industry was highly competitive, with many established players vying for market share. However, O'Neil believed that Walmart's low-cost business model and focus on customer service would enable it to outperform its competitors over the long term.

Over the next decade, O'Neil's investment in Walmart proved to be a wise decision. The company grew rapidly, opening new stores across the country and expanding into new markets. Walmart became a dominant player in the retail industry, with a market capitalization of over $100 billion by the late 1990s.

When analyzing stocks, he relied on several key indicators to identify stocks with strong momentum and growth potential. Here are some of the key indicators that O'Neil used to analyze stocks:

1. Earnings Per Share (EPS): One of the most important fundamental indicators for O'Neil was a company's earnings per share. He looked for companies with strong EPS growth rates over the past few quarters and years. Companies with strong EPS growth rates are often expected to continue to grow in the future and have strong momentum.

2. Sales Growth: O'Neil also looked at a company's sales growth rate, as this can be a good indicator of a company's potential for future earnings growth. He looked for companies with strong sales growth rates over the past few quarters and years.

3. Relative Price Strength: Another key technical indicator that O'Neil used was relative price strength. This measures how well a stock has performed compared to other stocks in the same industry or sector. O'Neil looked for stocks that were outperforming their peers in terms of price strength.

4. Volume: He also paid close attention to trading volume, as this can indicate whether there is strong interest in a stock. He looked for stocks that had strong trading volume, as this can be a sign of momentum.

5. Chart Patterns: He used technical analysis to look for chart patterns that indicate a stock is likely to continue its upward trend. He looked for stocks with cup-and-handle patterns or stocks that had formed a strong base before breaking out.

Another example of O'Neil's success with momentum investing is his investment in Baidu Inc., a Chinese search engine company. In 2006, O'Neil purchased shares of Baidu at a price of around $100 per share. Baidu had recently gone public, and O'Neil saw the potential for the company to grow in the rapidly expanding Chinese market. As Baidu's earnings and stock price continued to grow, O'Neil held onto his shares, eventually selling them in 2011 for a profit of over $900 per share.

His successful application of momentum investing principles has resulted in significant profits over the years. However, it's important to note that not all of his investments have been successful, and O'Neil has also experienced losses at times. Nonetheless, his ability to identify stocks with strong momentum and his willingness to cut losses quickly when necessary has helped him to achieve success in the market.

CHAPTER 3. RICHARD DRIEHAUS

"One market paradigm that I take exception to is: Buy low and sell high. I believe far more money is made by buying high and selling at even higher prices."

Richard Driehaus

Richard Driehaus is a well-known investor and philanthropist who has made a significant impact in the world of finance over the course of his career. Born in 1942, Driehaus grew up in a middle-class family in Chicago and developed an early interest in business and finance.

After completing his undergraduate studies at DePaul University, Driehaus began his career in finance as a stockbroker, working for a number of different firms in Chicago. During this time, he developed an interest in investing and began to experiment with different investment strategies.

In the 1970s, Driehaus founded his own investment firm, Driehaus Capital Management, with the goal of developing an investment approach that focused on identifying emerging trends and investing in companies that were well-positioned to benefit from those trends. This approach, which would later be known as momentum investing, would become the cornerstone of Driehaus's investment philosophy over the years.

In the early days of his career, Driehaus faced a number of challenges as he worked to establish his firm and develop his investment approach. He struggled to attract clients at first, and he often had to rely on personal connections and word-of-mouth referrals to build his business.

Despite these challenges, Driehaus remained committed to his vision, and he continued to refine his investment approach over time. He began to focus on identifying companies that were experiencing strong positive momentum in the market, and he developed a number of tools and techniques to help him identify these trends:

1. Relative Strength: One of the key tools that Richard Driehaus used to identify stock trends was relative strength. Relative strength is a measure of how well a stock is performing relative to the broader market. Driehaus believed that stocks with high relative strength were more likely to continue to perform well in the future. He used a number of technical indicators, such as moving averages and momentum oscillators, to identify stocks with high relative strength.

2. Earnings Growth: He also believed that earnings growth was an important factor in identifying stocks with strong momentum. He looked for companies that were experiencing strong earnings growth and had the potential to continue to grow earnings in the future. Driehaus would often invest in companies that were experiencing earnings surprises, or that had recently announced positive earnings guidance.

3. Chart Patterns: Driehaus was a firm believer in technical analysis, and he used a number of chart patterns to help him identify stock trends. He looked for stocks that were breaking out of consolidation

patterns, such as triangles and rectangles, and he also looked for stocks that were forming bullish continuation patterns, such as flags and pennants.

4. Sector Analysis: He recognized that stock trends often occur within sectors or industries, and he used sector analysis to identify these trends. He would often focus on sectors that were experiencing strong earnings growth or that were benefiting from broader macroeconomic trends.

5. Stop Losses: Driehaus used stop losses to manage risk in his portfolio. He would set stop losses at predetermined levels, and he would sell a stock if it fell below these levels. This helped him to limit losses and preserve capital in his portfolio.

Driehaus has been successful in using this strategy over the years, and his investment philosophy has helped him generate significant returns on his investments. In the mid-1990s, Driehaus invested in Dell, which was then a relatively unknown company. He paid around $1.50 per share and purchased a significant stake in the company. Driehaus believed that Dell's direct-to-consumer model, focus on customization, and efficient supply chain management made it a strong player in the growing computer industry. He also noted the company's strong earnings growth and positive earnings surprises as reasons to invest.

Over the next several years, Dell's stock price soared as the company's revenues and earnings continued to grow. Driehaus took advantage of the strong momentum in the stock and sold his position for a substantial profit. He reportedly earned more than ten times his initial investment, with the stock reaching a peak of over $50 per share.

He also made a successful investment in Intel, a leading manufacturer of computer processors, in the early 2000s. He paid around $16 per share and made a significant investment in the company. Driehaus recognized that the technology sector was undergoing significant changes at the time, with the growth of the internet and the increasing demand for high-speed processing power. He believed that Intel was well-positioned to benefit from these trends due to its strong research and development capabilities and dominant market position.

Additionally, Driehaus noted that Intel's earnings growth had been consistently strong, with positive earnings surprises in multiple quarters. He also recognized the company's strong balance sheet and dividend history as reasons to invest.

Over the next several years, Intel's stock price continued to climb as the company's earnings growth remained strong. Driehaus was able to take advantage of this momentum, selling his position for a significant profit. He reportedly earned more than three times his initial investment, with the stock reaching a peak of over $70 per share.

However, Driehaus also faced some setbacks as a result of his momentum investing strategy. For example, during the dot-com bubble in the early 2000s, many of the technology stocks that he had invested in experienced significant losses as the market corrected. As a result, Driehaus lost a significant portion of his net worth during this time.

Despite these setbacks, Driehaus continued to believe in the potential of momentum investing, and he remained committed to the strategy over the long term. He continued to invest in stocks that exhibited strong positive momentum, such as Google and Amazon, and he was able to generate significant returns from these investments over time.

In the mid-2010s, he made a successful investment in Netflix, the streaming video company, based on his assessment of the company's long-term growth potential. Driehaus recognized that the traditional TV model was undergoing significant changes with the growth of streaming services. He saw Netflix as a leading player in this space, with a growing subscriber base and a focus on producing original content. He believed that the company's strong brand, growing library of original programming, and global expansion plans made it a strong investment opportunity.

He also noted that Netflix's earnings growth had been consistently strong, with positive earnings surprises in multiple quarters. He recognized the company's strong financials, with a solid balance sheet and a healthy cash flow. Additionally, Driehaus noted that Netflix was benefiting from the trend towards cord-cutting, as more and more consumers were switching to streaming services.

Driehaus made his initial investment in Netflix in 2014 when the stock was trading around $60 per share. Over the next several years, Netflix's stock price soared as the company's revenues and earnings continued to grow. Driehaus took advantage of the strong momentum in the stock and continued to increase his position. He reportedly earned more than five times his initial investment, with the stock reaching a peak of over $400 per share.

After making a considerable profit, Driehaus decided to sell his position in Netflix. He observed that the stock's valuation had become stretched and the company was facing increasing competition from other streaming services in a crowded market. While he had experienced success with the investment, Driehaus believed that it was crucial to recognize when to take profits and move on to other opportunities.

CHAPTER 4. JOHN W. HENRY

"You can't win in any sport without heavily concentrating on revenue generation. You have to be relentless in that regard if you are going to be able to afford the kind of players you need to compete at the highest level."

John W. Henry

John W. Henry was born on September 13, 1949, in Quincy, Illinois. He grew up in a middle-class family and attended Victor Valley High School in California. In his early years, Henry was interested in sports and played baseball and football in high school.

After graduating from high school, Henry attended Victor Valley College and later transferred to the University of California, Riverside, where he earned a degree in agriculture. However, Henry's interests shifted towards finance and investing, and he began reading books on the subject in his spare time.

In the early 1970s, Henry moved to Chicago and started his career as a commodities trader. He worked for various trading firms and gained experience in the futures markets. However, Henry struggled to make consistent profits and was eventually fired from his job.

Undeterred, Henry decided to start his own trading firm and

founded John W. Henry & Company in 1981. The company initially focused on trading in the futures markets, using computer algorithms to identify trading opportunities. Henry's innovative use of technology and data analysis helped him gain an edge in the market and led to the firm's success.

In the late 1980s, Henry began applying the Momentum Investing strategy to his investments, buying and selling stocks based on their momentum. This strategy proved to be highly successful, and the firm's assets under management grew rapidly.

Henry recognized that Whirlpool, a manufacturer of home appliances such as refrigerators, washing machines, and dryers, was a well-established company with a strong brand reputation and a dominant market share in its industry. He also noted that the company was experiencing solid financial performance, with consistent revenue growth and strong profitability.

He purchased shares of Whirlpool Corporation in 2018 at an average price of $148.94 per share. As of 2021, the stock price had risen to over $240 per share, resulting in a total return of over 60% for Henry's investment.

In addition to his success in finance, Henry has also been involved in sports ownership. In 1991, he made the decision to purchase the Florida Marlins baseball team for a reported $95 million. At the time of Henry's purchase, the Marlins were a relatively new expansion team that had struggled to gain a foothold in the competitive baseball market. Despite their struggles, Henry saw the potential for the team to succeed and set out to build a winning franchise.

Henry brought a unique perspective to sports ownership, drawing on his experience as a successful investor and entrepreneur. He recognized that building a successful sports team required a similar approach to building a successful business - identifying key areas of strength, investing in talent, and strategically managing resources.

Under Henry's ownership, the Marlins began to experience significant success on the field. In 1997, the team won its first World Series championship, thanks in part to key acquisitions such as pitcher Kevin Brown and outfielder Moises Alou.

However, Henry's tenure as the owner of the Marlins was not without controversy. He clashed with local officials over plans to build a new stadium and faced criticism from fans for his decision to sell off key players following the team's championship win.

In 1999, Henry made the decision to sell the Marlins to a group of investors for a reported $158 million. While he had achieved his goal of building a winning franchise, Henry recognized that sports ownership was a challenging and unpredictable business.

John W. Henry and his investment group, New England Sports Ventures, made a notable sports ownership investment when they purchased the Boston Red Sox baseball team for $700 million. Henry saw the team as an undervalued asset with the potential for significant growth if managed correctly. Applying his Momentum Investing strategy, he believed that he could improve the team's performance on the field and increase its value off the field.

His strategy was to invest heavily in the team's roster, bringing in high-performing players who were in the prime of their careers. He also invested in the team's infrastructure, building a state-of-the-art training facility and upgrading Fenway Park, the team's historic home stadium. These investments paid off on the field, as the Red Sox won three World Series championships under Henry's ownership, in 2004, 2007, and 2013.

Off the field, Henry's investments in the team's infrastructure and marketing helped increase the team's revenue significantly. In 2002, the team's revenue was $162 million, but by 2010, it had grown to $302 million. This growth in revenue was driven by increases in ticket sales, merchandise sales, and sponsorships, which were all directly related to the team's success on the field.

In 2011, after nearly a decade of ownership, Henry decided to sell the Boston Red Sox. He believed that the team's value had peaked and that it was time to cash out his investment. In addition, he wanted to focus on his other business ventures, including his financial management firm, John W. Henry & Company.

Henry sold the team for $1.1 billion, which was a significant return on his initial investment of $700 million. This profit was largely driven by the team's success on the field and its growth in revenue off the field, which had increased the team's overall value.

One of his most notable sports ownership investments was his acquisition of Liverpool Football Club in 2010. At the time of the acquisition, John W. Henry's investment group, Fenway Sports Group, paid £300 million (approximately $477 million USD) for Liverpool Football Club. The purchase was made after the previous owners, Tom Hicks and George Gillett, defaulted on their loans, which led to a legal battle and the club being put up for sale.

His investment in Liverpool was based on his belief that the club was undervalued and had the potential for significant growth. He saw the club as a valuable asset with a rich history and a dedicated fan base, and he believed that with the right management and investment, the team could be successful both on and off the field.

Under Henry's ownership, Liverpool has experienced a significant transformation. The team has won several major trophies, including the UEFA Champions League, the Premier League, and the FIFA Club World Cup. In addition, the club has seen significant growth in its commercial revenue, with sponsorships and merchandise sales increasing.

As of 2023, Liverpool Football Club is valued at approximately £2.25 billion (approximately $2.83 billion USD), which is a significant increase from the £300 million that Henry paid for the club in 2010.

CHAPTER 5. DAVID HARDING

"The idea that markets are always rational, that they perfectly reflect all knowable information and always produce in some sense the right price. It treats economics like a physical science when, in fact, it is a human or social science. Humans are prone to unpredictable behaviour, to overreaction or slumbering inaction, to mania and panic."

David Harding

David Harding was born on February 9th, 1961, in London, England. He grew up in a middle-class family and attended a comprehensive school in the London borough of Bromley. Harding was an intelligent student, and after finishing school, he went on to study physics at the University of Sussex.

After completing his degree, Harding began his career as a research scientist at Racal Electronics, a British electronics company. However, after a few years, Harding decided to pursue a career in finance and joined Bank of America as a financial analyst.

While working at Bank of America, Harding became interested in quantitative investing and started to develop his own trading algorithms. In 1990, Harding left Bank of America and co-founded AHL, a quantitative hedge fund, with two colleagues. AHL was one of the first hedge funds to use computer algorithms to make investment decisions.

Under Harding's leadership, AHL quickly became one of the most successful hedge funds in the world. By the late 1990s, the fund had grown to manage over $1 billion in assets and had delivered annualized returns of around 20%.

However, in 1997, Harding left AHL to start his own hedge fund, Winton Capital Management. Winton Capital Management initially started as a small operation with just a handful of employees, but it quickly grew into one of the most successful hedge funds in the world.

At Winton Capital, Harding continued to use quantitative investing strategies, including momentum investing, to achieve strong returns for his investors. He also developed new investment strategies, such as trend-following and statistical arbitrage, to further diversify the fund's portfolio.

Today, Winton Capital Management manages over $20 billion in assets and is one of the largest hedge funds in the world. Harding is widely regarded as one of the most successful quantitative investors of all time, and his pioneering work in the field of computerized trading algorithms has paved the way for a new generation of quantitative investors.

In 2007, Winton Capital made a substantial investment in Apple Inc., a technology company that was undergoing a transformation under the leadership of Steve Jobs, at a cost of around $12 per share. The investment turned out to be a profitable one for Winton Capital, and it was driven by several key factors.

Firstly, David Harding believed that Apple was a company with a strong brand and a loyal customer base. He recognized that Apple's products were in high demand, and that the company had a reputation for innovation and quality. He believed that Apple's products were so distinctive and well-designed that they would continue to attract consumers for years to come. This view was supported by Apple's financial performance at the time, which was strong and indicated a positive outlook for the future.

Secondly, Harding also recognized the potential of Apple's ecosystem. Apple had created a closed system that allowed it to control the hardware and software used in its products. This system allowed Apple to create a seamless and integrated user experience that was difficult for competitors to replicate. Harding believed that Apple's ecosystem would continue to attract and retain customers, and that this would translate into continued growth and profitability for the company.

Thirdly, Harding also took into account the broader technological and economic trends that were shaping the industry at the time. He recognized that the rise of mobile technology and the internet were creating new opportunities for companies like Apple. He saw that Apple was well-positioned to capitalize on these trends and to continue to innovate and grow.

Finally, Harding's investment in Apple was driven by a quantitative approach to investing. Winton Capital Management uses algorithms and data analysis to identify investment opportunities and make investment decisions. In the case of Apple, the firm used its quantitative models to analyze Apple's financial performance, market position, and other relevant factors. This approach allowed Winton Capital to make a well-informed investment decision based on objective data and analysis.

Over the next few years, Apple's stock price continued to rise, and by 2012, Winton Capital had sold its shares at a price of around $680 per share. This represents a significant return on investment for Winton Capital, with the shares increasing in value by over 5,500% over the five-year period.

David Harding used a variety of key indicators to analyze stocks and identify potential investment opportunities. These key indicators are based on mathematical models and statistical analysis and are used to identify stocks that are showing strong momentum or have the potential to generate strong returns.

One of the key indicators that Harding used is price momentum. Price momentum is a measure of the stock's recent price performance and is based on the idea that stocks that have shown strong price performance in the recent past are likely to continue performing well in the future. Harding would analyze a stock's price momentum by looking at the stock's price chart and identifying trends in the stock's price movement over time.

Another key indicator that Harding used is earnings momentum. Earnings momentum is a measure of a company's recent earnings performance and is based on the idea that companies that have shown strong earnings growth in the recent past are likely to continue growing their earnings in the future. Harding would analyze a company's earnings momentum by looking at the company's financial statements and analyzing trends in the company's revenue and earnings growth over time.

Harding also used technical indicators to analyze stocks. Technical indicators are based on mathematical formulas and are used to identify trends in a stock's price movement. Some of the technical indicators that Harding used include moving averages, relative strength index (RSI), and Bollinger Bands. Moving averages are used to smooth out a stock's price movement over time and identify trends in the stock's price movement. RSI is used to identify when a stock is overbought or oversold, and Bollinger Bands are used to identify when a stock's price is moving outside of its normal trading range.

In addition to these key indicators, Harding also used other quantitative analysis techniques, such as factor analysis and statistical arbitrage, to identify investment opportunities. Factor analysis involves identifying underlying factors that are driving stock prices, such as changes in interest rates or market volatility. Statistical arbitrage involves identifying pricing discrepancies between related securities and taking advantage of these discrepancies to generate profits.

Another example of how Harding applied momentum investing can be seen in his investment in Amazon.com Inc. In 2014, Winton Capital bought shares of Amazon at a cost of around $300 per share. At the time, Amazon was experiencing strong momentum due to the growth of its e-commerce business and the success of its Amazon Prime subscription service. Over the next few years, Amazon's stock price continued to rise, and by 2020, Winton Capital had sold its shares at a price of around $3,100 per share. This represents a significant return on investment for Winton Capital, with the shares increasing in value by over 1,000% over the six-year period.

CHAPTER 6. ANDREAS CLENOW

"Extremely few people have ever become financially independent by trading their own account. You become financially independent by trading other people's money. The gist of this argument is that if you trade your own money, you have a limited upside and take all the risk. A highly skilled professional trader is likely to see returns in the range of 12-18% per year over time, with occasional drawdowns of about three times that."

Andreas Clenow

Andreas Clenow is a prominent quantitative trader and author who has achieved significant success in the financial industry over the years. Clenow was born in Switzerland in 1972 and developed an early interest in finance and trading.

His first experience in the financial industry came in the early 1990s when he began working at a Swiss investment bank. He started out in a junior role but quickly moved up the ranks, eventually becoming a senior trader responsible for managing a significant portfolio of assets.

In the late 1990s, Clenow moved to London to work for a major investment bank. There, he continued to develop his skills as a quantitative trader and gained a reputation as an expert in systematic trading and portfolio management.

Starting his own hedge fund in the early 2000s, Clenow utilized his expertise in quantitative analysis and trading strategies to create a successful fund that produced strong returns for his investors. Over the years, Clenow continued to refine his approach to trading and investment management. He developed a systematic, quantitative approach that focused on identifying stocks with strong positive momentum and using a disciplined investment strategy to capitalize on these trends:

1. Market Trends: He pays close attention to market trends to identify stocks that are likely to perform well. He uses a variety of technical indicators to analyze trends and determine which stocks are likely to trend upwards.

2. Risk Management: Clenow places a strong emphasis on risk management when investing in stocks. He uses a variety of strategies to minimize risk, including diversification, stop-loss orders, and position sizing.

3. Fundamental Analysis: While he is primarily known for his quantitative analysis skills, he also pays attention to fundamental factors when making investment decisions. He considers factors such as earnings growth, dividend payouts, and valuation metrics to identify stocks that are likely to perform well over the long term.

4. Volatility: Clenow recognizes that volatility is an important factor when investing in stocks. He uses volatility-based indicators to determine the optimal entry and exit points for his trades, helping to minimize risk and maximize returns.

5. Backtesting: He uses backtesting to evaluate the performance of his trading strategies. He uses historical data to test his strategies and determine

their effectiveness, helping him to refine his approach and identify new opportunities.

6. Automation: Clenow believes in the power of automation when it comes to investing in stocks. He uses automated trading systems to execute his trades, helping to eliminate emotion and improve consistency.

7. Portfolio Optimization: He uses advanced mathematical models to optimize his portfolio and maximize returns while minimizing risk.

In addition to these indicators, Clenow also looks at a range of other factors when analyzing a stock, including its industry sector, its competitive position, and the overall market environment. He uses a combination of quantitative analysis and expert judgment to evaluate these factors and identify potential investment opportunities.

Clenow has also become a well-known author, publishing several books on systematic trading and investment strategies. His books, which include "Following the Trend" and "Stocks on the Move", are widely regarded as essential reading for anyone interested in quantitative trading and momentum investing.

He has achieved significant success in applying this approach to his trading. For example, he has reported earning returns of over 40% in some years by applying momentum investing strategies. This success has come from a combination of careful analysis of the markets and disciplined execution of his investment strategy.

In early 2017, Clenow made a significant investment in NVIDIA. His decision to invest in the company was based on several factors, including the growing demand for GPUs in various industries, such as gaming, artificial intelligence, and data center applications. NVIDIA is a leader in the GPU market and has a strong reputation for innovation and quality. Coupled with the company's solid financials, this made it an attractive investment opportunity for Clenow.

His investment in NVIDIA was also influenced by his investment philosophy, which emphasizes quantitative analysis and the use of trading systems. Clenow has developed a systematic approach to investing, which he calls "Swing Trading with a Twist". This approach involves using quantitative analysis to identify stocks that are likely to trend upwards and employing a set of trading rules to manage risk and maximize returns.

Clenow purchased NVIDIA stock at a price of $103 per share. Using his quantitative analysis and trading rules, he managed his position, which resulted in a strong return on his investment. The stock continued to trend upwards, reaching an all-time high of $615 per share in late 2020. This translates to an estimated gain of approximately 495% for Clenow on his investment in NVIDIA.

Another example of Clenow's success with momentum investing is his investment in the biotech company Biogen, which he purchased in 2010. At the time, Biogen was a relatively unknown company with a market capitalization of around $12 billion. However, Clenow saw potential in the company's strong pipeline of drugs and its focus on developing treatments for neurodegenerative diseases.

Clenow purchased Biogen at a price of around $54 per share, and held onto the investment for several years as the company's stock price continued to rise. In 2015, he sold the investment at a price of around $380 per share, earning a significant return on his initial investment.

CHAPTER 7. MICHAEL MARCUS

"If you don't stay with your winners, you are not going to be able to pay for the losers. I think the leading cause of financial disablement is the belief that you can rely on the experts to help you. Investing requires an intense personal involvement."

Michael Marcus

Michael Marcus is widely known as one of the greatest traders of all time. He is a renowned trader and is famous for turning $30,000 into over $80 million in just 20 years.

He was born in 1945 in New York City and grew up in a family of modest means, and his father was a salesman. Marcus did not have a formal education in finance or trading, and he started his trading career as a commodities broker in the early 1970s. He worked at a brokerage firm where he learned about the commodities markets and trading.

Marcus was always interested in the financial markets, and he was an avid reader of financial publications. He became interested in trading after reading an article in Fortune magazine about a successful trader who had made a fortune trading soybeans. This inspired Marcus to pursue a career in trading.

In 1972, Marcus made his first trade in the commodities markets. He bought a soybean futures contract and made a small profit.

This success gave him the confidence to continue trading. He began to study the markets and developed his own trading strategies.

His early trading days were not without their challenges. He lost money on several trades and had to borrow money from his mother to cover his losses. However, he was determined to succeed and continued to refine his trading strategies.

In the early 1980s, Marcus had his big break. He was introduced to legendary trader Ed Seykota, who mentored him and helped him develop his trading skills. Seykota taught Marcus about risk management, trend following, and the importance of discipline in trading.

Under Seykota's guidance, Marcus became a highly successful trader. He started his own trading firm and began trading for clients. He was one of the first traders to use technical analysis and trend following techniques in his trading. His trading philosophy was simple but effective. He believed that successful trading was a combination of three factors: a sound trading strategy, proper risk management, and the ability to execute trades with discipline. He also believed in the importance of constant learning and self-improvement.

One of Marcus's notable investments was in Berkshire Hathaway, the investment firm led by Warren Buffet. In the early 1980s, Marcus purchased Berkshire Hathaway shares for around $300 per share. He held onto the shares for several years, as the price steadily increased. Eventually, he sold his shares for over $1,000 per share, earning a significant profit. He recognized the upward trend in the price of the stock and capitalized on it.

As a momentum investor, Michael Marcus focused on analyzing a stock's price trends and movements in order to identify buying and selling opportunities. He believed that prices tended to continue to move in the same direction over a certain period of time, and that by identifying these trends, he could capitalize on them for profit. Some of the key indicators that Marcus used to analyze a stock included:

1. Moving Averages: Moving averages are used to smooth out fluctuations in a stock's price over time. By looking at the stock's moving average over a certain period of time, Marcus could determine whether the stock was trending up or down.

2. Relative Strength Index (RSI): The RSI is a technical indicator that measures the strength of a stock's price movement. Marcus used this indicator to identify overbought and oversold conditions in a stock, which could signal a buying or selling opportunity.

3. Volume: Marcus also analyzed a stock's trading volume, as he believed that high trading volume indicated strong market interest in the stock. High volume could be a signal of a trend reversal or confirmation of an existing trend.

4. Price Patterns: He paid close attention to price patterns in the stock's chart, looking for patterns that indicated bullish or bearish sentiment. For example, a stock that forms a "head and shoulders" pattern could indicate a bearish reversal, while a "cup and handle" pattern could indicate a bullish continuation.

5. Market News: Marcus also considered market news and events that could affect the stock's price. This could include company earnings reports, economic data releases, or geopolitical events that could impact the stock's underlying fundamentals.

In the early 1980s, Michael Marcus made a bold move by investing heavily in Compaq Computer Corporation's stock, which was then a relatively unknown player in the computer industry. Marcus was a well-known commodities trader at the time and had a reputation for making successful trades based on his ability to identify trends in the market. However, his investment in Compaq was a departure from his typical approach to trading, which focused primarily on commodities.

Based on his analysis of the personal computer market, Michael Marcus invested in Compaq stock because he believed that the company had the potential to dominate this rapidly growing industry. Marcus saw that the company had a strong management team, a clear strategy for growth, and a commitment to innovation. He also believed that the company had a competitive advantage in the form of its ability to deliver high-quality products at a lower cost than its competitors.

His decision to invest in Compaq was also based on his analysis of the company's financials. He saw that the company had a strong balance sheet and was generating significant cash flows from its operations. He also believed that the company was undervalued by the market and that its stock price would rise as the company continued to grow and gain market share.

Another factor that influenced Marcus's decision to invest in Compaq was his experience as a trader. He had seen many companies come and go in the commodities market, and he recognized that Compaq had the potential to be a long-term winner. He also saw that the company's stock price was likely to be volatile in the short term, but he was willing to tolerate this volatility in order to achieve significant long-term gains.

Marcus's investment in Compaq turned out to be a prescient move. The company went on to become one of the dominant players in the personal computer industry, and its stock price soared in the years that followed. He purchased shares of Compaq at around $10 per share and held onto them as the price continued to increase. Eventually, he sold his shares for over $100 per share, earning a massive profit.

In the mid-1980s he invested in IBM stock, which was then considered a blue-chip company and a mainstay of the technology industry. Marcus paid around $100 per share for the stock, which was considered expensive at the time.

The rationale behind his investment in IBM was based on his analysis of the company's financials, market position, and prospects for growth. He recognized that IBM had a strong balance sheet and was generating significant cash flows from its operations. He believed that the company's financial strength would help it weather any challenges that might arise in the future.

He was also impressed by IBM's market position as the dominant player in the computer industry. He saw that the company had a significant competitive advantage and believed that its strong brand and reputation would enable it to maintain its market position and continue to generate profits in the years to come.

In addition, Marcus recognized IBM's commitment to innovation. He saw that the company was investing heavily in research and development and was constantly introducing new products and services to the market. He believed that IBM's focus on innovation would enable it to stay ahead of its competitors and continue to grow in the years to come.

Finally, Marcus saw that IBM's stock price was undervalued by the market at the time. He believed that the company's potential for growth was not fully reflected in its stock price, and he saw significant upside potential in the stock.

Marcus's investment in IBM turned out to be a wise move. The company continued to dominate the computer industry, and its stock price rose significantly, generating substantial gains for Marcus. He held onto the stock for several years and sold it at a price of around $200 per share, earning a profit of around 100% on his investment.

In 1990, Marcus retired from trading at the age of 45. He had made a fortune from trading, and he wanted to spend more time with his family and pursue other interests. However, he continued to be involved in the financial industry and started a hedge fund in 1996.

CHAPTER 8. ED SEYKOTA

"The elements of good trading are: 1, cutting losses. 2, cutting losses. And 3, cutting losses. If you can follow these three rules, you may have a chance."

Ed Seykota

Ed Seykota, born in 1946, is a renowned trader who is widely recognized for his contribution to the development of trend following and technical analysis. Seykota's early days were marked by his passion for mathematics and interest in the stock market, which ultimately led him to become one of the most successful traders of his time.

His fascination with the stock market began during his teenage years when he became interested in reading financial newspapers and analyzing the stock market. This led him to pursue a degree in Electrical Engineering at MIT, where he was exposed to the principles of probability theory and statistics, which helped him develop a quantitative approach to trading.

After completing his degree, Seykota began his career as an analyst at a brokerage firm in Chicago. It was during this time that he discovered the work of Richard Donchian, a pioneer in the field of trend following. Donchian's approach to trading was based on the idea that markets trend and that traders can make profits by identifying and riding these trends.

Seykota was fascinated by Donchian's approach and decided to develop his own trading system based on these principles. He began testing his system on historical data and soon found that it was highly effective in identifying trends and making profitable trades.

His trading system relied heavily on technical analysis, which involves studying price charts and other market data to identify trends and patterns. He used a variety of technical indicators, such as moving averages, to help him identify trends and determine when to enter or exit trades.

In the early 1970s, Seykota moved to California and became a member of the newly formed Commodities Corporation, which was founded by two legendary traders, Richard Dennis and Bill Eckhardt. At Commodities Corporation, Seykota was able to refine his trading system and develop new techniques for identifying trends and managing risk.

Seykota's trading success at Commodities Corporation soon caught the attention of other traders and investors, and he began managing money for outside clients. His track record of consistently delivering high returns on investment earned him a reputation as one of the best traders in the business.

One example of Seykota's success with momentum investing is his investment in the stock of a company called MCI. In the early 1980s, MCI was a telecommunications company that was challenging AT&T's monopoly in the US. Seykota saw that the stock of MCI had been showing a steady upward trend in price, and decided to invest in it. He bought the stock at around $6 per share, and held onto it as it continued to rise in price. Eventually, he sold his shares for around $90 per share, making a profit of more than 1,400%.

Seykota used a variety of technical indicators to analyze stocks and determine when to enter or exit trades. Some of the key indicators he used include:

1. Moving Averages: A trend-following indicator that helps traders identify the direction of the trend. Seykota used moving averages to identify support and resistance levels, as well as to determine when a trend was likely to reverse.

2. Relative Strength Index (RSI): The RSI is a momentum indicator that measures the strength of a stock's price action. Seykota used the RSI to identify overbought and oversold conditions in a stock, which can help traders determine when to enter or exit a trade.

3. Bollinger Bands: A volatility indicator that helps traders identify periods of high and low volatility. Seykota used Bollinger Bands to identify when a stock was likely to break out of a trading range, which can provide a profitable trading opportunity.

4. Fibonacci Retracement: A technical analysis tool that helps traders identify potential levels of support and resistance. Seykota used Fibonacci retracement levels to identify potential entry and exit points for trades.

5. Price Action: Price action refers to the movement of a stock's price over time. Seykota used price action analysis to identify key levels of support and resistance, as well as to identify potential breakout or reversal patterns.

In addition to these technical indicators, Seykota also used fundamental analysis to evaluate the financial health and growth prospects of a company. This involved analyzing financial statements, industry trends, and other market data to determine whether a stock was undervalued or overvalued.

In the early 1990s he bought Amgen stock at around $15 per share and held onto it for several years, during which time the stock experienced significant growth. Seykota's investment in Amgen was based on several key factors.

Firstly, he recognized the emerging growth potential of the biotech industry, given the increasing demand for healthcare and the aging of the population. He believed that Amgen was well-positioned to capitalize on this trend.

Secondly, Seykota was impressed by Amgen's strong track record of innovation and product development. The company had a pipeline of new drugs and therapies in development, and Seykota believed that these products had the potential to be highly successful in the market.

Thirdly, Seykota was impressed by Amgen's financial performance. The company had a solid balance sheet and was consistently profitable, with strong cash flows and a low debt-to-equity ratio. He believed that these financial metrics were a good indicator of the company's long-term viability and growth potential.

Finally, Seykota recognized that Amgen was a leader in its industry and had a strong competitive advantage. The company's products were highly regarded by healthcare professionals and patients, and Amgen had established strong relationships with key players in the healthcare industry. Seykota believed that these factors would help to protect Amgen's market position and allow the company to continue to grow and expand over the long term.

His investment in Amgen turned out to be a wise decision, as the stock price soared over the years. He reportedly sold his Amgen shares for around $100 per share, earning a considerable profit.

CHAPTER 9. 10 MAJOR LESSONS FOR GROWTH INVESTING

Momentum investing is a popular investment strategy that involves buying assets that have been trending in price and selling assets that have been losing value. The idea behind momentum investing is that assets that have been performing well will continue to perform well in the short term, while assets that have been performing poorly will continue to underperform. Here are ten major lessons about momentum investing:

1. Momentum investing is a short-term strategy. Momentum investing works best in the short term, typically between three and twelve months. While momentum investing can be profitable over longer periods, the returns tend to be lower.

2. Momentum investing requires patience. To be successful with momentum investing, you need to be patient and wait for the right opportunities to present themselves. It's important not to get caught up in short-term fluctuations and to stay focused on the long-term trend.

3. Momentum investing involves risks. Like any investment strategy, momentum investing involves risks. There is always the possibility of unexpected

events that can cause a stock to lose value, even if it has been performing well.

4. Momentum investing requires diversification. To reduce the risks associated with momentum investing, it's important to diversify your portfolio. This means investing in a variety of assets, including stocks, bonds, and other investments.

5. Momentum investing can be done with exchange-traded funds (ETFs). One of the easiest ways to get started with momentum investing is by investing in ETFs that track momentum-based indexes.

6. Momentum investing requires discipline. To be successful with momentum investing, you need to have a disciplined approach to buying and selling assets. This means sticking to a set of rules and not getting caught up in emotions.

7. Momentum investing requires monitoring. To be successful with momentum investing, you need to monitor the performance of your portfolio regularly. This means tracking the price movements of your assets and making adjustments when necessary.

8. Momentum investing is not a guarantee of success. While momentum investing can be profitable, there are no guarantees. Like any investment strategy, there is always the possibility of losses.

9. Momentum investing is based on market psychology. The momentum investing strategy is based on the idea that market participants tend to overreact to news and events, causing assets to become overvalued or undervalued.

10. Momentum investing requires a long-term view. While momentum investing is a short-term

strategy, it's important to have a long-term view of your investments. This means considering the fundamentals of the companies you invest in and their potential for future growth.

In conclusion, momentum investing can be a profitable investment strategy, but it requires discipline, patience, and diversification. By following these ten lessons, you can increase your chances of success with momentum investing.

ABOUT THE AUTHOR

JACK FISHER is a former engineer, entrepreneur, and investor. He lives in California, United States with his fiancé and two children. Jack loves educating and inspiring other investors and entrepreneurs to succeed and live the life of their dreams.

www.ingramcontent.com/pod-product-compliance
Lightning Source LLC
Chambersburg PA
CBHW071118220526
45467CB00004B/1937